STEAM JOBS IN
MARKETING

Curtis Ross

Educational Media

rourkeeducationalmedia.com

Before Reading:

Building Academic Vocabulary and Background Knowledge

Before reading a book, it is important to tap into what your child or students already know about the topic. This will help them develop their vocabulary, increase their reading comprehension, and make connections across the curriculum.

1. *Look at the cover of the book. What will this book be about?*
2. *What do you already know about the topic?*
3. *Let's study the Table of Contents. What will you learn about in the book's chapters?*
4. *What would you like to learn about this topic? Do you think you might learn about it from this book? Why or why not?*
5. *Use a reading journal to write about your knowledge of this topic. Record what you already know about the topic and what you hope to learn about the topic.*
6. *Read the book.*
7. *In your reading journal, record what you learned about the topic and your response to the book.*
8. *After reading the book complete the activities below.*

Content Area Vocabulary
Read the list. What do these words mean?

analytics
campaign
consumers
nonprofits
product
research analyst
search engine
traffic
viral

After Reading:

Comprehension and Extension Activity

After reading the book, work on the following questions with your child or students in order to check their level of reading comprehension and content mastery.

1. *How can social media help promote a marketing idea?* (Summarize)
2. *How does math play a role in marketing?* (Infer)
3. *What do marketers use data for?* (Asking questions)
4. *What does ROI stand for? Explain why it is important when marketing a product.* (Text to self connection)
5. *What role does sociology play in marketing?* (Asking questions)

Extension Activity

With a group of friends, pick an item or something that interests you. Come up with a way to market your item by making a marketing plan. Assign each friend a different role like the ones discussed in the book. Work together to see how your marketing plan is progressing. When you are finished, test your plan on family, friends, or your classmates!

Table of Contents

What Is Marketing?

We're all familiar with advertising. We see advertisements on websites. They pop up regularly when we're watching TV. They line the roads on billboards.

Many people think marketing is just another word for advertising. But advertising is just one of the elements that makes up a marketing **campaign**.

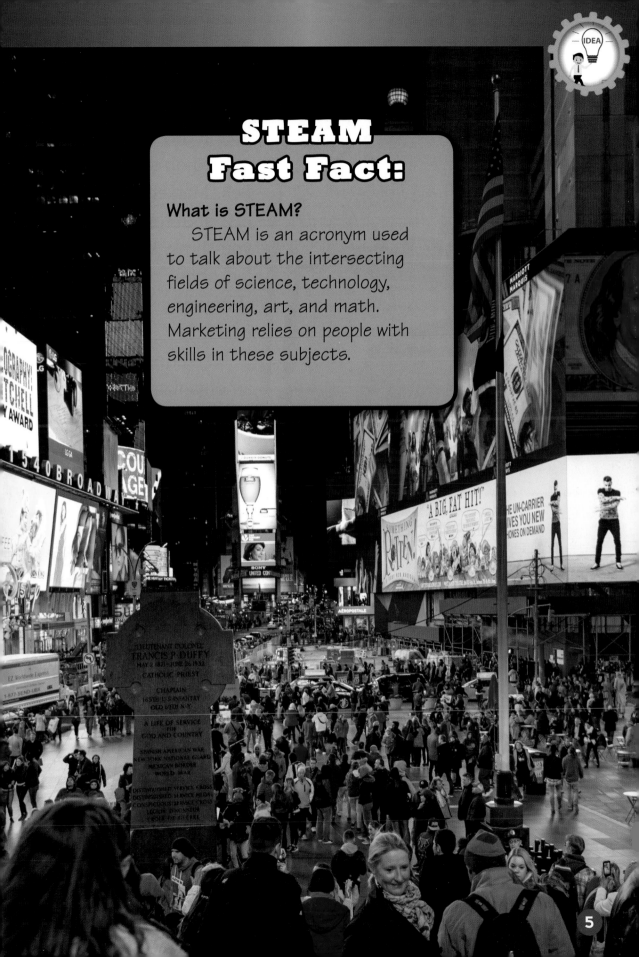

STEAM Fast Fact:

What is STEAM?

STEAM is an acronym used to talk about the intersecting fields of science, technology, engineering, art, and math. Marketing relies on people with skills in these subjects.

IDEA

An advertisement tells you about the new mega-burrito on sale at Taco Bell. Marketing influences just about everything you think, know, and feel about the fast-food restaurant.

Marketing is everything an organization does to make itself known to, and hopefully loved by, the public.

STEAM Fast Fact:

Marketers must know their markets. Nike found itself in hot water in the Middle East when the flame logo on one of its shoes was thought to resemble the Arabic word for Allah.

It's everything involved with a **product**, from the original idea through its creation until it reaches the consumer.

STEAM Fast Fact:

Marketing doesn't always work the way it's intended.

In 1985, Coca Cola advertised a change to its recipe and got a huge response from **consumers**—demanding a return to the original formula!

Businesses aren't the only organizations that market themselves. Sports teams, entertainers, charities, and colleges also employ professionals to help them find an audience and create a good impression.

Some people may think of marketing as more of an art than a science. In the past, this may have been true.

STEAM Fast Fact:

The great thing about marketing is that you can seek out a position that suits your interests, whether that's marketing business, government, sports, entertainment, or anything else. Just about every organization needs marketing—and marketers.

Sure, a little psychology might be used to figure out—or guess, really—what would appeal to consumers, but there was a time when marketers mostly went with their gut instincts.

Thanks to advances in technology, modern marketers have access to massive amounts of data to help them determine how to best promote their organizations.

In fact, there is so much data coming in—from social media, search engines, credit card swipes and other sources—that a successful marketing business must have employees with backgrounds in science, technology, engineering, and math. They also need people with the artistic flair and creativity to turn that data into something that appeals to consumers.

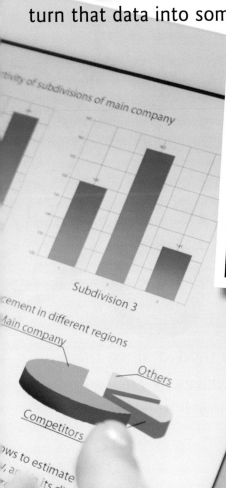

tivity of subdivisions of main company

Subdivision 3

cement in different regions

Main company

Others

Competitors

ows to estimate

	Last	Chg	%Chg	Vol B	Bid
○ SET ○ TFEX				---- Active List ----	
	34.50	+1.25	+3.76%	534,800	34
	4.96	+0.02	+0.40%	24,900	4
	239.00	+5.00	+2.14%	103,200	239
	130.00	+2.00	+1.56%	41,500	130
	374.00	+5.00	+1.36%	80,700	373
	2.60	+0.06	+2.36%	7,111,600	2
	422.00	+4.00	+0.96%	75,650	422
	150.50	+3.00	+2.03%	242,200	150
	52.75	+1.75	+3.43%	861,000	52
	58.50	+1.75	+3.08%	397,100	58
			34.50	Vol/Value(K)	

STEAM Fast Fact:

Marketing isn't always about making a profit. Sometimes it's just about exposure. The band Radiohead got lots of publicity in 2008 when its album "In Rainbows" was first released only as a download from the band's website. Fans could pay any price they wanted, or just download it for free.

Reason

Logic Mind

Maths

Language

Black & White Vision

Sense of Time

You may have heard people say they are right-brained or left-brained. It's a way of classifying themselves as creative (right-brained) or better with math and science (left-brained).

Well, marketing requires you to be whole-brained! Marketers must know how to use data to decide when, where, how, and to whom they should market. They also have to use creativity to make their audience respond positively.

Art ♪ ♫ Music

Colors

Creativity

Intuition

Emotions

How a product or person is portrayed visually is an important element of the marketing process. Forty-six percent of marketers say photography is critical to their marketing strategies. Color photos and art increase people's willingness to read marketing content by 80 percent, according to researchers.

Marketing Math

Math-savvy marketers have to crunch the numbers regularly. What are they doing when they're in math mode?

Marketers conduct polls and surveys to gather a variety of information, such as:

- who is or isn't using their product
- what customers like and don't like about the product
- the ages of people buying the product
- how much money their product's consumers earn and where they live

Analyzing, interpreting, and presenting this statistical data so others can understand it is integral to the process marketers use to develop their campaigns. The information helps the marketing team determine what kind of advertising campaign to create, and where advertisements should run.

A product's marketing campaign budget is carefully considered from many angles, from the value of exposure to new customers to the actual sales the company hopes it will generate.

Marketers must carefully calculate return on investment (ROI) for a product's campaign. ROI measures the amount of return on an investment compared to the investment's cost. In other words, how much money is spent on marketing compared to the value of the sales it generates.

Science & Tech Savvy

Sociology, the study of groups of people and their habits and histories, is a science used by marketers. It helps marketers know who wants or uses their product.

STEAM Fast Fact:

In early 2007, Barack Obama was a little-known U.S. senator from Illinois. By late 2008, he'd been elected president. Much of his success was due to his use of social media marketing on YouTube and Facebook.

Marketers study habits of groups of people. These groups are often divided by demographics such as age, gender, country of origin, and even specific likes and dislikes, from sports to music. The more marketers know about their customers, the better they are able to choose how and where to market to them.

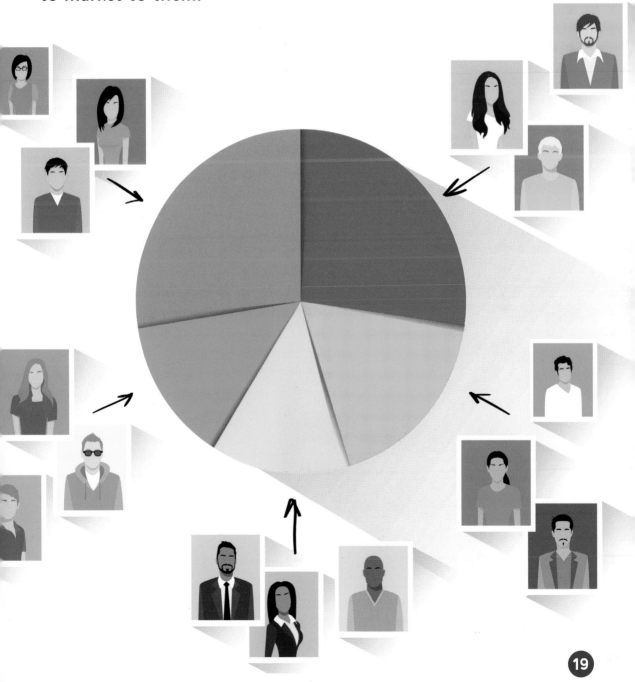

Technology might be the most important STEAM element in marketing. Consumer technology gives marketers new channels with which to reach customers, while new web tools provide marketers with data that helps them do their jobs better.

The Internet continues to create new ways to market. Mobile technology lets marketers reach customers as they're shopping. Each social media platform offers a new way to reach potential consumers, from 140-character messages on Twitter to stylish photos on Instagram.

Just as important for marketers is the technology that lets them track how well their campaigns are working.

Tools such as Google **Analytics** give marketers information on how many visitors their web pages get, how long visitors stay on a page, where web **traffic** is coming from and much more.

nalytics/

Google Analytics

Home   Features   Learn   Partners

Standard Repor

What Do Marketers Market?

Just about any organization that has any interaction with the public markets itself.

You probably notice the marketing of consumer items the most. These are things you buy, such as food, clothes, cars, sporting goods, smartphones, and video games.

STEAM Fast Fact:

Do your own marketing! When Coca Cola began selling soda in China, it had no Chinese translation. Shop owners stepped in, choosing Chinese language characters that could be pronounced "ko-ka-ko-la" but translated into bizarre phrases such as "bite the wax tadpole."

The companies that make the parts and ingredients that are used in those consumer goods engage in marketing too. They market to the companies that sell you those completed products.

Charities and **nonprofits**, such as the Red Cross and the American Cancer Society, market themselves so people know about the services they offer.

They also market themselves so that people will donate money to help them provide those services.

Universities market themselves in order to attract students. Religious organizations market themselves to encourage people to attend their churches.

Any organization that wants the public to know about it uses marketing to get its message to the public.

STEAM Marketing Jobs

Just as all sorts of organizations need marketers, there are all sorts of different jobs that can be described as marketers.

Almost all marketers use elements of STEAM—science, technology, engineering, art, and math—in some combination.

If you think of a marketing office as a laboratory, then the marketing manager would be the lead scientist. The market **research analyst** would be his laboratory assistant.

STEAM Fast Fact:

When you market can be as important as what you market. Social media marketers know that Facebook, Twitter, and LinkedIn each have peak traffic periods when posts are most likely to be seen.

The market research analyst gathers large amounts of data using surveys, questionnaires, and opinion polls. They also must gather data on consumers, the organization's competitors, and market conditions. Then they interpret the data, which the marketing manager will use to make decisions.

STEAM Fast Fact:

Analysts use bar graphs, pie charts, and other models to illustrate and compare data from different sources. These charts help them compare a product's performance from different time periods, or see how it performed against a competitor's product.

The market research analyst's work helps an organization decide what products or services the public wants. They also try to find out who will want the product or service—young or older people? Males or females? People who live in the city or in the suburbs?

With this information, the marketing team, with the marketing manager leading the way, does what any scientist does.

First, they form a hypothesis. Example: "This new brand of soda will appeal to males ages 18 to 25 who like extreme sports."

Then they test the hypothesis. One way might be to give away samples of the soda to fans attending a skateboarding competition.

The test is designed to answer questions such as: Did the subjects like the product? Why or why not?

Then, based on the results, they accept, reject, or refine the initial hypothesis.

Technology

There probably isn't a single marketing job that doesn't involve technology. Each element of Internet marketing—social media, email, homepages and so on—requires someone with expertise in that area.

Market research analysts use computer software such as Office Excel to create the charts and graphs that illustrate the data they collect.

Art directors use programs such as Photoshop to create the visual image the organization wants to present to the public.

An organization's visual image is part of its online marketing statement. Digital marketing engineers ensure that an image is just as striking whether it's viewed on a desktop, laptop, tablet or smartphone.

Digital marketing engineers are the marketers who have the most direct connection to technology. They must be familiar with different brands and devices to ensure that marketing messages are effective regardless of the platform. Designers make the content attractive, but engineers make sure the content arrives that way on the user's device, free of technical glitches and easy to navigate.

Engineering

Engineers use math and science to build systems and find solutions to problems. Digital marketing engineers are no exception. They design and build digital marketing plans that use the web to reach consumers with information about a product or organization.

Digital marketing engineers are more directly involved with the technical side of marketing than many other marketers. They ensure that marketing messages are effective on websites, in emails, on various platforms and on various devices.

STEAM Fast Fact:

Computer science is vital for these engineers. They must be able to grasp the formats and codes necessary to make the organization's message work on desktops, tablets, laptops, and smartphones.

e" width="300">
">

</script>

←— 300 px

←——— 800 px ———→

←— 500 px —→

←250

←—200 px—→

This requires engineering skills, computer science knowledge, and the creativity to make everything work together AND be compelling to the consumer.

Arts

Some brands are recognizable even if you don't see their name. When you see the swoosh, you know it's Nike. The golden arches? McDonald's. Artists who work in marketing may not be represented in museums, but their work potentially can be seen by millions of people all over the world.

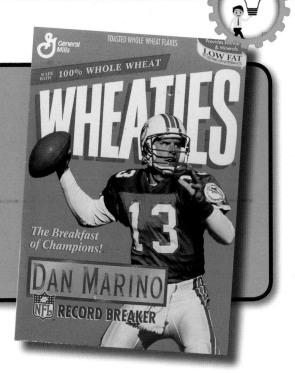

General Mills

TOASTED WHOLE WHEAT FLAKES

Provides Vitamins & Minerals
LOW FAT

MADE WITH 100% WHOLE WHEAT

WHEATIES

The Breakfast of Champions!

DAN MARINO

13

NFL RECORD BREAKER

STEAM Fast Fact:

Wheaties cereal has marketed itself as "The Breakfast of Champions" since 1934. It promotes that slogan by picturing athletes on its box.

Art directors are the marketers responsible for the way an organization appears visually. Art directors are concerned with everything visual, big or small. They'll choose a photo or illustration that will appear on a huge billboard, and they'll decide which font to use for the fine print of a product's packaging.

Choosing colors and fonts is serious business for a marketing art director.

Art directors are responsible for the visual image an organization uses to capture the public's attention.

They are responsible for the overall look of a marketing campaign, as well as all the little details that will be combined to make up that look. Art directors work with marketers from other departments to determine how the organization wants to be portrayed visually.

A store that sells trendy clothes to teens might use splashy, colorful graphics, while an insurance company probably would go for something more subdued, or serious.

Photographers, graphic artists, and digital animators are among the artists who might work in marketing.

Math

Numbers are a big part of marketing. How well did a product sell? How old are the people who buy it? How much will people pay for it? How many hits did our website get? How many shares did our social media post get?

Market research analysts use math constantly in their work. They must analyze large amounts of data and use that information to predict what consumers want, who those consumers are, and what their competitors are likely to do.

SEO technicians rely heavily on math to perform their duties. SEO stands for "**search engine** optimization." SEO technicians devise ways to make their organization's web pages show up on Google, Yahoo, Bing, and other search engines.

STEAM Job Facts

Marketing Director

Important Skills: math, computer science, creativity, interpersonal and communication skills

Important Knowledge: analysis, business law, management, economics

College Major: marketing, advertising or journalism

Market Research Analyst

Important Skills: analysis, critical thinking, communication, math, statistics

Important Knowledge: statistics, research methods, economics, consumer behavior

College Major: market research

Art Director

Important Skills: creativity, communication and leadership, time management

Important Knowledge: art, graphic design, photography, art history

College Major: fine arts

Digital Marketing Engineer

Important Skills: leadership, analysis, engineering

Important Knowledge: Internet, social media, web design, software, coding, HTML

College Major: marketing, computer science

SEO Technician

Important Skills: analysis, math, statistics

Important Knowledge: Internet, social media, coding, HTML

College Major: marketing, computer science

Director of Marketing Science

Important Skills: communication, analysis, critical thinking, advanced analytic techniques

Important Knowledge: analytics tools, metrics, statistics, research methods, data mining, statistical design, modeling, and testing

College Major: computer science, math, statistics, economics

Glossary

analytics (an-uh-LIT-iks): information gotten from analyzing data and statistics

campaign (kam-PAYN): an organized action in order to achieve a particular goal

consumers (con-SOO-mers): people who buy and use a product

nonprofits (non-PRAH-fits): charities or other organizations that don't operate for the purpose of profiting

product (PRAH-duct): an item for sale to consumers

research analyst (RE-serch AHN-al-ist): someone who studies and analyzes data

search engine (SERCH IHN-jin): a website that directs users to other sites based on keywords

traffic (TRAH-fic): visitors to a website

viral (VI-ruhl): Internet content that is shared by users

Index

Show What You Know

1. What does SEO stand for?

2. Has the Internet had any effect on marketing? How?

3. What are the "5 P's" of marketing?

4. Is marketing strictly for people who love numbers and technology? Explain.

5. What scientific steps does a market research analyst use?

Websites to Visit

www.themarketingstudent.com

http://bizkids.com

www.teachingkidsbusiness.com/business-basics-marketing.htm

About the Author

Curtis Ross is a writer and editor who's written for *The Tampa Tribune, Creative Loafing* and other print and online publications, in addition to his role as a content marketing assignment editor. He graduated from the University of Alabama and still yells "Roll Tide!" quite often. He is married and has three children who love to remind him that he is older than the Internet.

Meet The Author!
www.meetREMauthors.com

PHOTO CREDITS: Cover: cartoon guy and cogs art © Keepsmiling4u, pie chart © Vextok; pages 4-5 © rmnoa357, pages 6-7 Taco Bell building © Ken Wolter, Coca Cola © MAHATHIR MOHD YASIN; pages 8-9 FIBA World cup © Natursports, computer © Rawpixel.com, university website © Rawpixel.com; pages 10-11 ipad © Pressmaster, stock market data © Peerawit, laptop © Rawpixel.com; pages 12-13 left and right brain illustration © carla castagno, whole-brained © iQoncept, magazines © Trong Nguyen; pages 14-15 laptop © Ditty_about_summer, feedback icon © iQoncept, ; pages 16-17 graphs © Nonwarit, scales © DRogatnev, sketched flow chart © faith; page 18 graph © Mushakesa, Obama Facebook page © Bakhur Nick, page 19 © ProStockStudio; pages 20-21 instagram shot © Tamisclao, twitter shot © 1000 Words; pages 22-23 Google Analytics shot © Ingvar Bjork, BMW showroom © Hadrian, Cola can © topnatthapon; pages 24-25 American Red Cross sign © 360b, American Cancer Society sign © SandiMako; page 26-27 computer with data analysis © angellodeco; pages 28-29 computer online reviews © Rawpixel.com, computer with graphs © Andrey_Popov; page 30 soda bottles © kzww, skateboarder © Sergei Bachlakov; pages 32-33 © Georgejmclittle; pages 34-35 © nonstick; pages 36-37 © everything possible, page 37 © Rudie Strummer; pages 38-39 McDonalds © jannoon028, Nike logo © rmnoa357, Wheaties box © Perry Correll, page 39 computer shot © scyther5; Pages 40-41 woman at computer © Rawpixel.com, guy with camera © Rido, using digital pen © Dikiiy; pages 42-43 sales report © safriibrahim, web traffic © donskarpo; SEO chart © dizain. All photos from Shutterstock.com

Edited by: Keli Sipperley

Cover and Interior design by: Nicola Stratford   www.nicolastratford.com

Library of Congress PCN Data

STEAM Jobs in Marketing / Curtis Ross
(STEAM Jobs You'll Love)
ISBN 978-1-68191-740-5 (hard cover)
ISBN 978-1-68191-841-9 (soft cover)
ISBN 978-1-68191-933-1 (e-Book)
Library of Congress Control Number: 2016932703

Printed in the United States of America, North Mankato, Minnesota

Also Available as:
ROURKE'S
e-Books